EVERYBODY POOPS
10 Million Pounds

Published in the United States by:
Ulysses Press
P.O. Box 3440
Berkeley, CA 94703
www.ulyssespress.com

ISBN: 978-1-61243-494-0
Library of Congress Control Number: 2015937557

Printed in the United States

10 9 8 7 6 5 4 3 2 1

Acquisitions editor: Keith Riegert
Project editor: Alice Riegert
Managing editor: Claire Chun
Proofreader: Renee Rutledge

EVERYBODY POOPS
10 Million Pounds

The Astounding Fecal Facts from a Day in the City

Text by Deuce Flanagan   **Illustrated by Valentin Ramon**

ULYSSES PRESS

WELCOME TO A WORLD OF POOP

Everybody on Earth produces roughly a pound of poop a day. In large cities around the globe, that can mean millions of pounds of poop flowing through urban sewers every single day. So what happens to all that human-made manure? And what did we do before sewers even existed? Grab yourself a porcelain seat and prepare to be blown out of the water. You're about to dive deep into the fascinating past, present and future of the human flush, including:

- How poop shaped civilization;

- The dirty history of the sewage system;

- What exactly happens after you flush;

- How New York City's poop ended up in Lamar, Colorado;

- How the poop you make may be growing the food you eat; and

- The incredible, dare we say magical, future of poop.

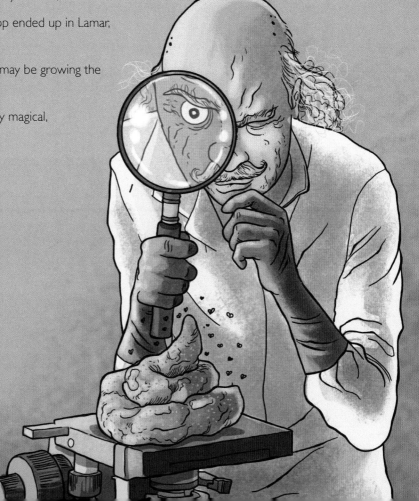

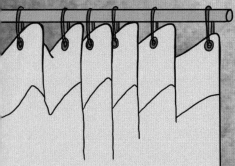

THE WORST OF POOP

So what is poop anyway? Well, friend, you might not know it, but poop can tell a whole lot about you: what you ate, what you're made of, how healthy you are and even how you feel emotionally. But if you really want to dig your hands in, poop is:

- 75% water you never absorbed

- 10% dead bacteria

- 10% fiber and undigested food

- 5% living bacteria

And it's that measly 5% living bacteria that causes so many problems. Ingesting the living parts of poop can end with a nasty case of giardia, typhoid fever, hepatitis, cholera, tapeworms and much, much more!

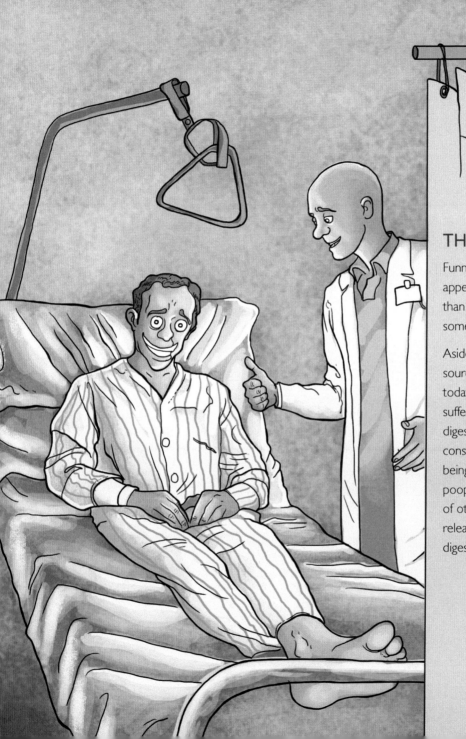

THE BEST OF POOP

Funny thing is that while poop appears to be nothing more than smelly waste, it actually has some remarkable benefits.

Aside from making great sources of fuel and fertilizer, today, poop helps people suffering from a range of digestive orders, including constipation, IBS and colitis, by being given as experimental poop transplants—capsules of other people's poop that release helpful bacteria into the digestive tract.

EVOLUTION OF THE DEUCE

You probably don't think about it at all, sitting high and mighty on your bleach-white toilet, but it took a lot of generations to get your bum perched on that pooper. Here's how it all went down:

Ⓐ The Furry Full Squat *(20 million years ago)*
Our forest-dwelling ancestors were, as you might imagine, pretty casual about things when it came to poop. In the primordial bush, all that was required was a soft shrub and a commodious squat.

Ⓑ The Caveman Crouch *(1 million years ago)*
As we evolved to stand up straight on two feet, taking a number two became more of a production. Nevertheless, we kept nearly the same pooping position as our fuzzy ancestors.

Ⓒ The Chamber Pot Plopper *(400 years ago)*
Amazingly, not that much changed over nearly a million years of Homo sapiens' evolution. Before toilets became the norm, most people simply moved the act indoors, depositing their nuggets in easily emptied chamber pots.

D The Contemporary Crapper *(Present)*

Today's prim-and-proper porcelain pooper may seem comfortable, but sitting actually makes things a lot harder. Toilet-users take over a minute longer to complete the deed than those using the squat.

E The Future Full Squat *(200 years from now)*

As science proves just how efficient, clean and natural the full squat is, don't be surprised to see future toilets take the act of #2 full circle to the squat.

A POOP'S HISTORY OF THE WORLD

Don't forget a fresh roll of toilet paper; you're about to take a journey back in time where you'll be hard-pressed to find a spare sheet. Heading back thousands of years, you'll encounter all sorts of ingenious, bizarre and disgusting ways our ancestors dealt with the #2. From pig latrines in China, poop-scooping gong farmers in Britain and communal crappers in Rome, the history of poop is, well, colorful. Let's take a plunge.

THE TREE OF CIVILIZATION

When humans decided to stop wandering around and first hunkered down in early settlements, we kept a lot of the easygoing traits of our nomadic forebearers. Among these qualities was crapping just about wherever we damn pleased. Low population density meant it went something like this: Pick a remote tree, declare it "toilet" and go on our merry way.

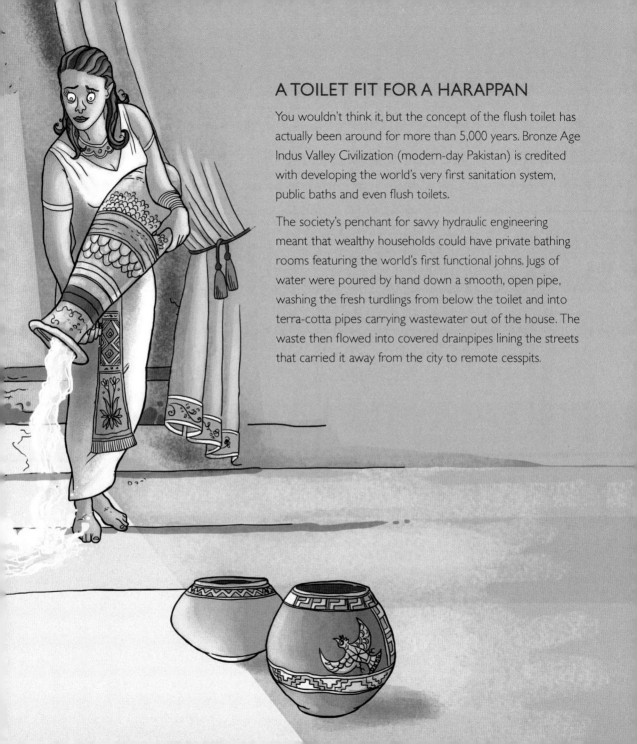

A TOILET FIT FOR A HARAPPAN

You wouldn't think it, but the concept of the flush toilet has actually been around for more than 5,000 years. Bronze Age Indus Valley Civilization (modern-day Pakistan) is credited with developing the world's very first sanitation system, public baths and even flush toilets.

The society's penchant for savvy hydraulic engineering meant that wealthy households could have private bathing rooms featuring the world's first functional johns. Jugs of water were poured by hand down a smooth, open pipe, washing the fresh turdlings from below the toilet and into terra-cotta pipes carrying wastewater out of the house. The waste then flowed into covered drainpipes lining the streets that carried it away from the city to remote cesspits.

DOING SOME BUSINESS
WHILE DOING YOUR BUSINESS

Taking a dump may be a private ritual today, but back
in Ancient Rome, it was a social event. Roman baths, with
their cold, warm and hot soaking tubs and refreshments for
sale, were *the* places to socialize. But why stop the party with
a nice soak? Roman baths also supported communal crappers with
rows of stone toilets that emptied into the sewer system below. "So, how
are your kids, Marcus?"

THE CRAPPIEST JOB IN HISTORY

Think "sewage treatment plant worker" is an undesirable job? Back in Tudor-era England, professional poop scoopers had it much worse. Gong farmers were in charge of removing all the human excrement from local cesspits. Allowed to work only at night, gong farmers toiled with shovel and bucket, waist-deep in ye olde deuces before spreading it on nearby fields as fertilizing night soil and trudging home to the outskirts of town—the only place they were allowed to live.

NEXT STOP, CANAL STREET

Humanity kept taking huge, smelly steps backward from the Middle Ages on, when they flushed the Roman practices of bathing, sewer construction and general sanitation straight down the nonexistent drain.

In early New York City, thousands of natural streams were turned into lazy man's sewers. As the dense settlement boomed, Manhattan's waterways brimmed with so much sewage and runoff that the streams slowed to a sludgy crawl and outbreaks of cholera and typhoid soon followed.

To drain the city's mounting sewage problem, wastewater was directed to a canal built along modern-day Canal Street. When the canal became a putrid mess, a crude roof was slapped over it to block out the stagnant cesspool. Out of nose, out of mind.

NOW SERVING ORGANIC, COLON-FED BACON

What is the world's most unappetizing waste management solution? The pig latrine. In rural Asia of yore, farmers designed their outhouses to feed directly into an attached pig trough. The pigs, in turn, lived a happy, slop-filled life—until, of course, they ended as stir-fried pork chop between the farmers' chopsticks.

(Accordingly, the Chinese character for "privy" also doubles as "pigsty.")

OLD-FASHIONED FECAL FACTS

The Crocodile Contraceptive—In ancient Egypt, contraceptive pessaries were crafted from honey, sodium carbonate and the dung of a crocodile. I think we're all getting that loving feeling.

Baby, Light that Fire—Egypt's love affair with crap went beyond crocodiles. Camel dung, an exceptionally fiber-rich animal poop, was used for millennia as a source of clean-burning fuel. Nothing quite like a fresh-baked loaf of bread infused with the aromatic smoke of camel crap.

Prognosis: Disgusting—Back in the Middle Ages, physicians used to diagnose their patients' ailments by taking a little nibble of a fresh specimen or two. Ironically, today, your poop can tell a lot about your overall health—you just don't want your doctor licking it to find out.

The Swiss Army Knife of Feces—Cows, domesticated back about 10,000 years ago, have supplied humans with one of our most versatile nature-made tools—cow pies. We have used cow dung to build houses (adobe bricks), fertilize our fields, heat our homes and even repel mosquitoes.

AIM OF THRONES

By now, you've probably gathered that the art of waste management has not gone particularly well throughout human history. Most of the 100 billion people who have ever lived on the planet have crapped in the woods, in little pots and into open, festering holes. Even a medieval king couldn't get a truly decent place to fire off a royal decree. And by the time the modern era rolled around, cities were booming and sewage was piling up. The world was on course for a filthy, stink-filled, sickening future. But hold onto your butts, things were about to change.

HOME, SWEET VICTORIAN HOME

Look familiar? This beautiful washroom is brought to you courtesy of the Industrial Revolution and Queen Victoria. By the age of industry, sanitation, a topic largely ignored for several hundred years, was once again something people actually thought about. And it was the spreading popularity of the common in-house flush toilet that began to transform society. With real sewage systems, cities were able to grow faster and larger and the world we now know took shape. Welcome to the modern era of the flushable turd.

THE BRILLIANT OUTHOUSE

The modern era of pooping really started with the outhouse. The design is simple, yet brilliant: close enough for convenience, far enough to keep those wafting scents at bay and deep enough (6 feet) to be scientifically genius.

Why 6 feet? Back in the day, we humans would designate some picturesque natural place as "toilet" and then deuce there day after day. Problem was that hookworms, poop-borne parasites, can crawl about 4 feet during their short lives, just enough to wriggle out of yesterday's droppings and back into your great-great grandfather's bare feet today. The pitted outhouse solved this by creating a Mount Everest–sized climb for poop's parasitic inhabitants.

IT'S ALL IN THE TRAP

While versions of the modern flush toilet date back as far as the 1500s (and early versions date back millennia), the greatest leap forward in modern toilet design belongs to a Scottish watchmaker and tinkerer named Alexander Cumming. Old Al came up with one simple, ingenious add-on to the indoor toilet—the S trap. Still used in toilets today, the snaking pipe fitting allowed for a pocket of sitting water to seal off the toilet bowl (and entire bathroom) from allowing in the noxious gases rising from the sewer below.

THE STINKING RIVER

The advent of flushable toilets in cities around the world may have done wonders for household hygiene, but that poop still had to go somewhere. Unfortunately, more often than not, that meant that urban poop ended up coming awfully close to city drinking water.

In the mid and late 1800s, Chicago faced this problem to a devastating degree. The city dumped its untreated sewage into the sluggish Chicago River, flowing directly into Lake Michigan, which doubled as the city's main supply of drinking water.

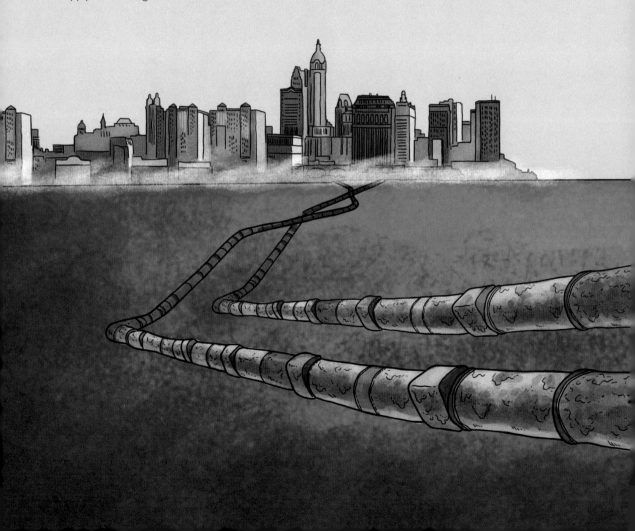

To combat the problem, the city tried numerous half-baked ideas. For instance, they built long intake tubes to draw clean water from the middle of the lake. Still the poop found a way to spread its filthy contaminants.

With waterborne diseases washing over the Windy City like an Illinois winter, Chicago's leaders came up with a totally, undeniably crazy idea: Instead of cleaning up the city's disgusting ways, it was deemed easier to just reverse the entire flow of the Chicago River. In what was the largest engineering undertaking at the time, Chicago steered the river away from Lake Michigan and sent it directly into the Missouri, straight toward St. Louis. All thanks to one big load of crap.

THERE'S TREASURE ON GUANO ISLAND

For all the money we humans have spent trying to get rid of poop, there's a lot of other dung that we pay handsomely to get our hands on. Guano, the sulfite- and nutrient-rich droppings of birds and bats, has long been prized for its use in gunpowder and fertilizer. But acquiring the crap can be remarkably dangerous. Cave spelunking and rock-scraping expeditions often end disastrously. Nevertheless, the dangers of this unappealing enterprise haven't stopped intrepid entrepreneurs—over 100 islands were claimed under the United States Guano Islands Act of 1856, which gave U.S. citizens the right to lay claim to any crap-covered rock that they could mine for droppings.

CRAPPY STARTUP COULD MEAN BIG BUSINESS

You might be surprised but there's actually a whole poop economy that's alive and well in our modern era:
A Herbivores like elephants produce very fibrous #2s, which some enterprising, bookish folk have started cleaning and pressing into high-quality paper. **B** Nightingale guano is the famous ingredient of many an expensive lotion. **C** Some of the priciest coffee you can find in the world has already been enjoyed once by something else—civets (a type of Indonesian weasel), to be precise. **D** Although not common anymore, the artificial vanilla and raspberry flavoring in your childhood desserts may have been derived from the anal glands of beavers. **E** Turns out, your body's unused food energy doesn't need to go to waste after all. Power plants are already burning what we flush. **F** Tired of beer that tastes like piss? Add a little civet or elephant poop coffee to a batch of beer and you've got a bottle of Big Konas from the Perrin Brewing Company. **G** Drinking water, reclaimed from your local sewage treatment plants, may be flowing right back through your tap soon.

A STEAMING CUP OF JAVA

Still looking for that perfect cup of Jo? Well look no further than Southeast Asia, because a few intrepid roasters have innovated what they would call "the world's best brew": elephant poop coffee. The process is simple: Coffee-loving elephants eat the beans, 15–70 hours later the partially digested beans come out the other end, workers sift through giant piles of elephant dung and the reclaimed beans are cleaned, roasted and brewed! This may seem absurd, but the elephant's digestive tract has enzymes that naturally strip the beans of their acidity, resulting in a surprisingly mellow flavor. Of course, this complicated, pachyderm-packed process comes with a hefty price: $50 a cup or $1,100 per kilo.

NEW YORK'S WAR ON POOP

There is probably no place on earth that is a better example of just how difficult it is to deal with poop than New York City. This city of skyscrapers, islands and 8.5 million people produces a whole lot of crap. But in just over a century, New York City went from a fetid, cholera-infested cesspool to one of the most highly efficient poop-processing metropolises in the world. What started with New Yorkers dumping their chamber pots directly into the street ended with millions of pounds of the Big Apple's highly processed poop on freight trains heading West. This is the fascinating story of how New York City took on a war on poop.

I'M ON THE HIGHWAY TO SMELL

Today, cities like New York boast incredible subterranean highways of poop. Every time you flush a turd, your bowl is emptied down your pipes, under your house and out to the sewer line where it joins all your neighbors' poops, dirty dishwater, soapy baths and local storm runoff. Your block's wastewater joins your whole neighborhood's liquidy crap, flowing down to larger mains and bigger and bigger pipes until it all ends up rushing into your local wastewater treatment center. It is truly a miraculous tangle of man-made streams and rivers that clean out the city every day. But it wasn't always like this. No, it was much, much worse.

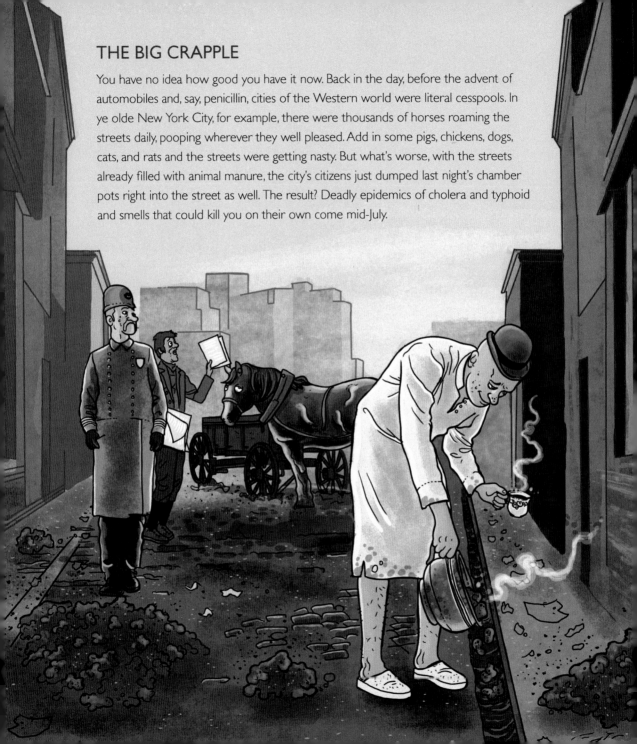

THE BIG CRAPPLE

You have no idea how good you have it now. Back in the day, before the advent of automobiles and, say, penicillin, cities of the Western world were literal cesspools. In ye olde New York City, for example, there were thousands of horses roaming the streets daily, pooping wherever they well pleased. Add in some pigs, chickens, dogs, cats, and rats and the streets were getting nasty. But what's worse, with the streets already filled with animal manure, the city's citizens just dumped last night's chamber pots right into the street as well. The result? Deadly epidemics of cholera and typhoid and smells that could kill you on their own come mid-July.

DESPERATE MEASURES

Facing unbelievable quantities of human feces, animal manure and garbage clogging Manhattan's street gutters, New Yorkers tried a variety of outlandish solutions to clean up the city. Taking a page from Asian farmers, they even tried employing roaming hordes of pigs to live off the rotting refuse. The pigs could have made a pretty decent sanitary department, except for the fact that they never seemed to develop a taste for poop.

THE GREAT TOILET WARS OF THE 1800s

In the latter half of the 1800s, New York's sanitation woes reached epic proportions. Every one of the five boroughs had its own sanitation president, each of whom quarreled with one another and had a work ethic only worth the pieces of crap he was supposed to be cleaning up. In 1895 it was reported that not one tenement building in the city of New York even had a *bath*, let alone functional indoor plumbing. Finally, desperate and out of homegrown ideas, the cities of Manhattan and Brooklyn combined forces and sent a commission to Europe to try to answer the question that New York couldn't figure out: How to deal with all that poop.

AN UNDERGROUND VENICE

Just as the 19th century began, New York City finally found its answer and got around to putting in a real sewer system. Today, the sewer system consists of over 6,500 miles of pipes and mains and moves 1.3 billion gallons of wastewater every single day. So where does all that sewage go?

A NICE DAY TO TAKE A FLOAT(ER)

The nearest river?! Unfortunately, while New York City got the sewer thing down, there was still the problem of what to do with the new river of underground sewage. Until as recently as the 1980s, New York City's sewage was dumped in its raw, unprocessed form directly into the East and Hudson Rivers. The fecal pollution from New York's booming, dense, population was so bad that, during unfortunate tides, raw sewage could wash up on the pristine Long Island beaches. But a solution was close at hand.

YOUR LOCAL CITY PARK...

Welcome to Riverbank State Park! Located on the Hudson side of Manhattan, this impressive 28-acre waterfront park and sports complex boasts an Olympic-sized swimming pool, ice skating rink, tennis courts and baseball and soccer fields. Add in a tree-lined promenade and grassy lawns and you've got a great place to spend a summer day. Except for one little, dirty secret...

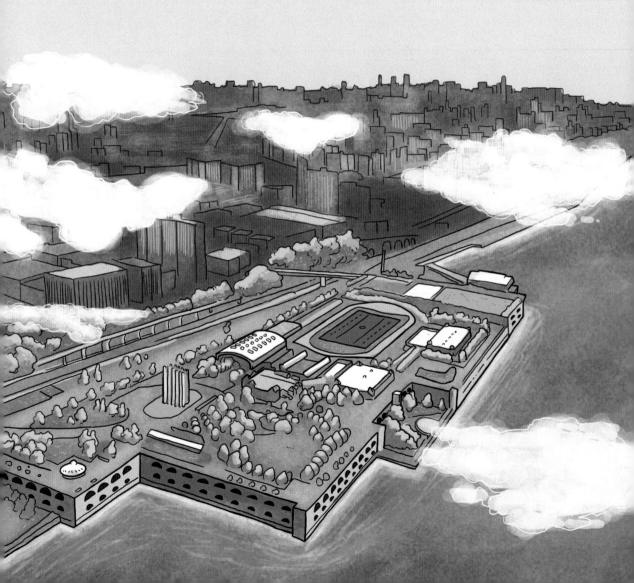

...MAY ACTUALLY BE A POOP PLANT

Before you take a bite of that delicious sandwich, you may want to know that this charming Manhattan park has been built on the roof of the North River Wastewater Treatment Plant. And beneath your picnicking feet, there are 125 million gallons of New York City's poop-filled water being processed right now. Turns out, those giant vent pipes are not there for decoration.

RETURN TO THE
BROWN LAGOON

Let's take a look at what exactly is going on below.
Every day, from Greenwich Village up to Washington
Heights, hundreds of thousands of toilet flushes flow through
the sewers beneath the city streets and over these brown,
cascading waterfalls. In this giant complex, a remarkable process takes
place that removes garbage, skims harmful oils, purifies filthy water and
separates out tons of solid sewage. Welcome to the poop factory.

THE BASICS OF SEWAGE TREATMENT

The Human Production Line: I poop, you poop, we all poop. A lot of poop.

Biosolids for Sale: After some final disinfection and treatment, biosolids are ready for a new home, like maybe, your garden.

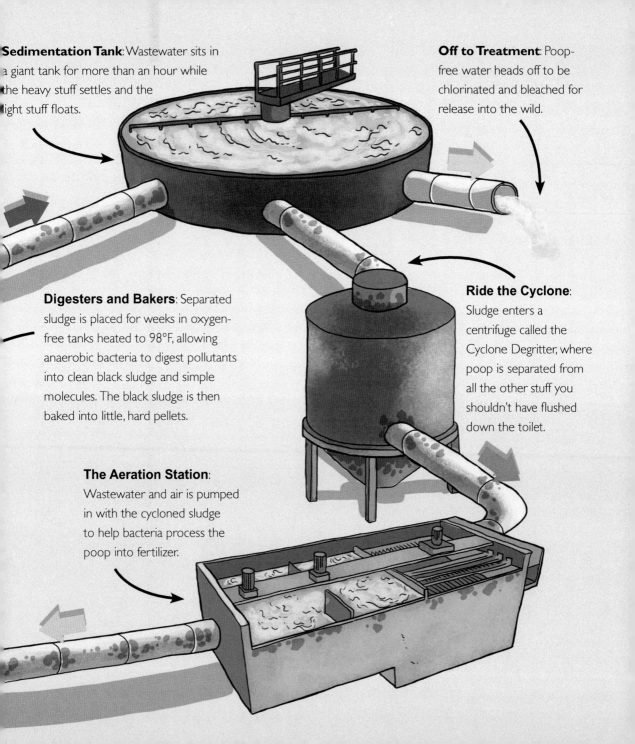

Sedimentation Tank: Wastewater sits in a giant tank for more than an hour while the heavy stuff settles and the light stuff floats.

Off to Treatment: Poop-free water heads off to be chlorinated and bleached for release into the wild.

Digesters and Bakers: Separated sludge is placed for weeks in oxygen-free tanks heated to 98°F, allowing anaerobic bacteria to digest pollutants into clean black sludge and simple molecules. The black sludge is then baked into little, hard pellets.

Ride the Cyclone: Sludge enters a centrifuge called the Cyclone Degritter, where poop is separated from all the other stuff you shouldn't have flushed down the toilet.

The Aeration Station: Wastewater and air is pumped in with the cycloned sludge to help bacteria process the poop into fertilizer.

OH, HOW THE TIMES HAVE CHANGED!

In most American cities, we've come a long way from when we used to just dump our feces into the nearest vacant area we could. Today, the wastewater flowing out of sewage plants that treat hundreds of thousands of people's poop is actually (kinda) mountain-spring-water fresh. So refreshing, so delicious.

OR MAYBE NOT…

Of course, in cities like New York, there is one caveat to getting that clean water—weather. The Big Apple (and many urban areas) combine storm drains and sewers into one big pipe headed toward the treatment pipe. That means that on a dry day, everything is peachy, but a good storm soaking means untreated sewage skips the cleaning process. In fact, roughly 40 billion gallons of untreated NYC sewage still spills into Manhattan's surrounding rivers and bays every year. Don't fall off that paddleboard!

WASTEWATER TREATMENT PLANT

THE ODIOUS CIRCLE OF LIFE

Live in a warm-weather city? Chances are your local sewage plant functions as its own marvelous ecosystem. In these tanks, small bacteria consume the poop's nutrients, larger bacteria eat the small bacteria, fungal mats form to feed off that bacteria. Fungus gnats arrive to this churning buffet. Spiders and insects arrive to dine on the engorged fungus gnats. And, finally, birds stop by to sample the selection of spiders.

ECOSYSTEM OF YOUR NIGHTMARES

Of course, if you live in a cold-weather or crowded city, your local sewage plant probably resembles your deepest nightmare. The enclosed, temperature-controlled indoor aeration tanks lock out any peckish birds, leaving spiders to rule the roost as tiny apex predators setting up house by the thousands and leaving thick blankets of webs on the ceilings.

JUST HOW MUCH POOP CAN NEW YORK MAKE?

Each day, New York City's 14 wastewater treatment plants produce 1,200 tons of poop-sludge biosolids. Finding that number hard to wrap your mind around? Let's put it another way: Every day, the poop (just poop) that piles up in New York City is the equivalent of 200 fully grown 16,000-pound African elephants entering the city. Think about it, without the incredibly efficient sanitation system, after just one year, there could be 75,000 poop elephants roaming Midtown.

WORLD'S BIGGEST TOILET BOWL

So what do you do with over 1,000 tons of poop sludge every day? New York being New York, the city found a nice place to dump it. Unfortunately for life in the Atlantic Ocean, until the Clean Water Act banned the practice in 1988, that dumping ground was about 100 miles off the East Coast. As you might expect, millions and millions of tons of toxic human feces settling to the ocean floor was not ideal. Some ocean animals went belly up, while others, like sea stars, urchins and sea cucumbers, found the creamy sludge delectable and had one big feast. Eventually, the poop toxins being devoured by these bottom-dwellers made their way up the food chain, ending up on ice in your local supermarket.

STOP AND SMELL THE ROSES

Along with banning ocean dumping, the Clean Water Act declared that, in order for New York City to repent for all the toxic crap it had dumped in the ocean for decades, the city had to find a beneficial use for all the waste it was producing. Well, turns out, nutrient-rich, human-made sludge makes a very potent agricultural fertilizer. Positive use, found.

Now, the name **New York City Sanitation Department Fecal Sludge** wasn't exactly going to fly off the shelves at the Home Depot in Omaha. So in what would have been the worst *Madmen* episode imaginable, a branding task force was formed and set about finding a way to turn New York's filthy poop into marketing gold. The task force considered some real gems, such as: **Powergrow, Black Gold, Bioslurp** and **ROSE** (Recycling of Solids Environmentally). In the end, the team settled on the vague, non-threatening name we know now: **Biosolids.**

IS YOUS LOOKIN' FOR A BIT OF THE BROWN?

Sadly, in the early 1990s, New York City's reputation was, well, pretty terrible. The City that Never Sleeps had just crawled its way out of the '80s and was still known primarily for its rats, drugs, prostitutes, graffiti, garbage and filth. So it's no wonder that when New York went out to peddle its biosolid waste to rural farmers in states like Alabama and Kentucky, they didn't get many buyers. In fact, they got zero buyers—they couldn't even give it away for free.

MIDNIGHT TRAIN TO THE ROCKIES

Finally, in what was almost a miracle last-ditch effort, New York City found a home for its biosolids. The tiny town of Lamar, Colorado, agreed to take the Big Apple's crap. All New York City had to do was find a way to transport an enormous amount of human waste some 1,600 miles from the Atlantic to the Rockies.

In April, 1992, a freight train loaded with processed Manhattan biosolids rolled out of New York and across the heartland of America. The few farmers in Lamar who had signed up to test out the biosolid fertilizer had no idea what to expect. Was it safe? Was it toxic? Would it burn a hole in the ground straight to hell?

BUMPER CRAPS

Turns out that New York City makes some darned fine fertilizer. The first farmers that used the biosolids reported bumper crops of wheat. So much wheat, in fact, that they broke their own harvest records. The biosolids even seemed to keep pests away from any field that had them. Before long, tens of thousands of acres of crops were planted with New York City's fertilizer and train shipments fanned out around the country.

YOU ARE WHAT YOU ATE

Which brings us back to this guy, about to take a bite of that delicious sandwich on top of the North River Wastewater Treatment Plant. You see, friend, hundreds of millions of loaves of bread were made from wheat grown in New York City's poop fertilizer. That means there is a chance that you are about to take a bite of bread that was grown, in part, thanks to the efforts of *you*. Ah, the great circle of poop!

DERAILING THE PORCELAIN EXPRESS

Alas, New York City's ambitions to make good with its own poop met a familiar fate to so many 21st century dreams—the Great Recession. In 2012, facing mounting costs and with cheaper alternatives, the city put an end to the cross-country poop shipments. Today, New York City's biosolids are mixed and used as earthen covering for landfills in the Northeast. Some things are just too beautiful for this world.

DON'T FLUSH THAT DREAM JUST YET

Is there a future for New York biosolids? As our population grows and environmental concerns mount, biosolids may still make a heroic comeback! After all, Milwaukee's own brand, Milorganite, a potent biosolid fertilizer first patented in the 1920s, can still be found at nurseries around the country. Who knows, someday, you may be able to choose from American-made biosolids from cities from sea to shining sea.

THE SCENT OF TOMORROW

New York City, and cities all around the world, sure have come a long way from their fetid, cholera-stricken pasts. Today, our toilets are clean and comfortable, toilet paper is soft and luxurious, and all the crap we produce disappears with the gentle push of a lever. How can it possibly get better? Well, in order to deal with the challenges of the future, like resource conservation and population increases, the way we poop and deal with the poop we make is about to change in ways you wouldn't begin to think possible. Let's take a look at the future of poop.

THE DAZZLING ZERO-WASTE FUTURE OF POOP

In the bathroom of tomorrow, you may just find everything working together in cyclical harmony. The water coming out of your shower may be water that was once in your toilet, now recycled and cleaner than ever. Enjoy hot showers? The energy that heats your water may be generated, in part, by the energy-rich poop you once manufactured yourself. In addition, new ergonomic toilets will require less aneurysm-inducing efforts and less wiping. Indeed, the future of how we go to the bathroom looks brighter than ever. But there are still some problems to solve.

DIRE STRAITS

The porcelain toilet in your bathroom may
look brand new, but the sewer lines beneath it
probably look like they're on the verge of imploding. In
dense, bustling cities around the country, the underground
sewer systems are ancient—many are even getting ready to
celebrate their bicentennial birthdays. As they age, their pipelines
begin to crumble, corrode and collapse with horrific results:
rotting stenches, contaminated drinking water and putrid sewage
explosions. The government estimates that an astounding 50% of
the country's sewers will be in dire need of repair by 2020.

WELCOME TO THE CRAMPED BATHROOM OF YOUR FUTURE

The world's poop problem really comes into focus when you consider that by 2050, the world's population will be approaching 10 billion, and 70% of us will live in cities. Some cities will boast populations greater than 50 million! If you consider that the Big Apple, a city of just 8.5 million inhabitants, produces 1.3 billion gallons of wastewater a day, just imagine what a megacity of 50 million will create. What on Earth could one of these cities do with, say, 7,000 tons of poop sludge every single day?

RAISE A GLASS TO THE OMNI PROCESSOR

The answer to tomorrow's poop woes may already be here. The Omni Processor, developed by the Bill & Melinda Gates foundation, could potentially solve the massive poop problem while bringing clean drinking water to the entire world. Currently, this building-sized power plant and water purifier has been scaled for use in developing countries that don't have the population density of, say, Shanghai. But the technology is marvelous and the possibilities limitless. The Omni Processor can take the raw sewage of up to 100,000 people a day, boil off and then recollect the water, and turn the dried solid waste into enough fuel to fully power the machine and purify the collected water through reverse osmosis.

FOREIGN OIL? WE HAVE DOMESTIC POOP

Your poop may also, soon enough, be shuttling you around town. The same chemistry that allows you to light a fart on fire also holds the potential for industrial-scale power generation. Deep in your bowels right now, bacteria are producing methane, a gas that can be bottled and used for power generation as biomethane. The first poop-fueled BioBus is actually already in service in West England and it's incredibly efficient. Just five days' worth of poop from your household can power the bus for an entire mile.

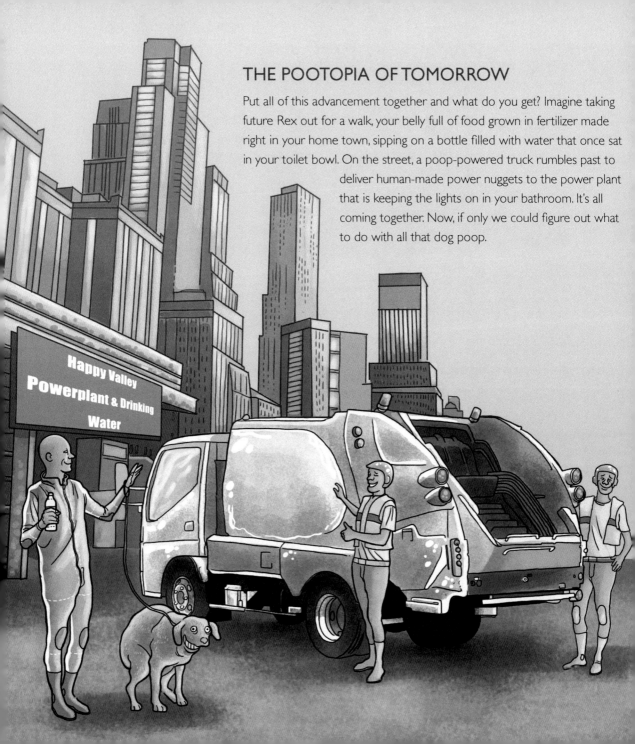

THE POOTOPIA OF TOMORROW

Put all of this advancement together and what do you get? Imagine taking future Rex out for a walk, your belly full of food grown in fertilizer made right in your home town, sipping on a bottle filled with water that once sat in your toilet bowl. On the street, a poop-powered truck rumbles past to deliver human-made power nuggets to the power plant that is keeping the lights on in your bathroom. It's all coming together. Now, if only we could figure out what to do with all that dog poop.

Happy Valley
Powerplant & Drinking
Water

MAKIN' MARS BARS

Finally, in the distant future, our Earthling descendants may spread out into the cosmos, bringing with them all our wonderful history, traditions, and bacteria. What will it be like to poop on another planet? There's a good chance that, having learned from our current environmental problems, everything we do in the cosmos will be more…reusable. With wastewater capture, purification, and biosolid recycling, our Martian great-great-great-grandchildren may drink the water they already drank and eat food grown in food they already ate.

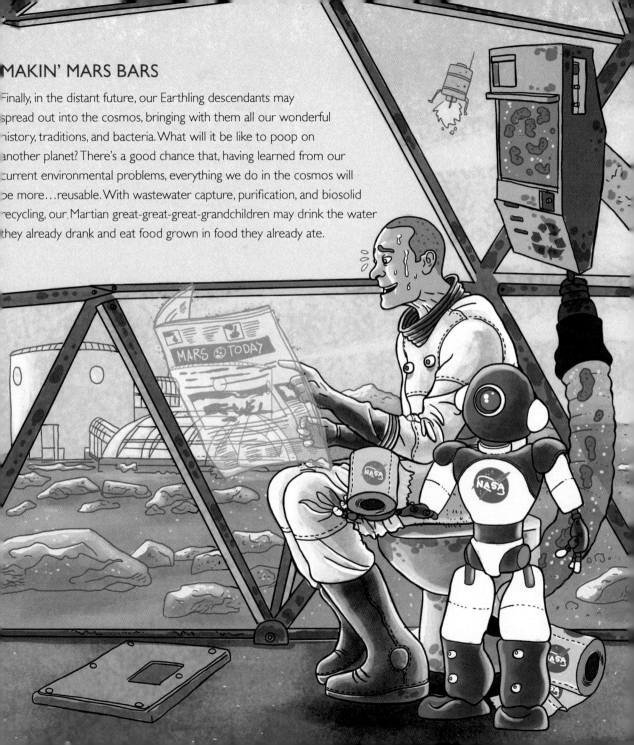

ABOUT THE AUTHOR AND ILLUSTRATOR

Deuce Flanagan, son of renowned New York plumber, Ham Flanagan, is a professor of Scatological Studies at the University of Minneapolis. Inspired by numerous children's books from his childhood that carefully taught him it was "okay to poop," Flanagan wrote the first-ever poop book for adults, *Everybody Poops 410 Pounds a Year*, winner of the fourth annual Golden Loaf Award for Feces-Related Literature. This is his second book.

Valentin Ramon is a professional illustrator living in London, UK. His work in the genre of wastewater-related illustration has oft been studied at the Art Institute of Mineola and his seminal work, "The Endless Constipations of General R.W. Medford," is in the permanent collection at the National Museum of Lavatory Arts.

• • •

Interested in more fascinating facts?
Try these other gems from the good folks at Ulysses Press:

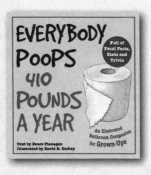

Everybody Poops 410 Pounds a Year: An Illustrated Bathroom Companion for Grown-Ups

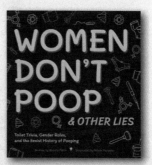

Women Don't Poop and Other Lies: Toilet Trivia, Gender Rolls, and the Sexist History of Pooping

Find out more at:
www.ulyssespress.com

Made in the USA
Columbia, SC
12 December 2020